Reaction Versus Response

Moving into Flow

Susie Armstrong

Copyright © 2023 Armstrong Press

All Rights Reserved.

No part of this publication may be reproduced, distributed, or transmitted in any form or by any means, including photocopying, recording, or other electronic or mechanical methods, without the prior written permission from the author, except in the case of brief quotations embodied in critical reviews and certain other non-commercial uses permitted by copyright law.

First Printing: January 2023

ISBN-13: 978-1-7356427-4-1

Susie Armstrong, MHR, LADC, LPC, C.HT

3829 N Classen Blvd. STE 200
Oklahoma City, OK 73112

(405) 921-9785

susiearmstrong.com

Instagram: @susie_armstrong

Susie is also the author of **SO.ARE.YOU**. A pathway to learning to love, accept, and be yourself through understanding the reflective mirrors in relationships and the world within and around you. Available for purchase at susiearmstrong.com or amazon.com

**Do you want Susie Armstrong to be the motivational speaker at your next event?
Call (405) 921-9785 or email your request to susiearmstrong88@gmail.com.**

Dedication

Mom, as always thank you for your love and support. I'm so grateful for you and all the rich experiences our relationship has provided. Seth, you're amazing! You motivate me every day to be a better version of myself. Thank you for choosing me to be your mother. And to all of the beautiful clients, mentees, friends, peers and random souls I've encountered on this journey, I thank you with all of my heart for walking the earth with me. I wouldn't have all of these beautiful stories of filled with contrast and wonder if it weren't for our connections. It's an honor walking the path with each and everyone of YOU!

Thank you and I love you.

About the Author

Susie Armstrong is a gifted writer, healer, actor, artist, and mother. She was born in Oklahoma City, Oklahoma and raised by a fun, talented, sassy mother, and a few interesting father figures. She loves connecting with loved ones, animals, nature, and other likeminded humans. Her passion is to continue to share love with the world through her writing, art, acting, and healing gifts. Susie is a Licensed Professional Counselor, a Licensed Drug and Alcohol Counselor, a Certified Professional Hypnotherapist, and a Certified EFT Practitioner. Susie is an expert in helping people implement change, by teaching them daily self-care tools to improve their ability to connect with themselves and others. In this book, Susie reveals tools and methods to help you learn to move from reacting into responding so you can effectively move into the natural flow of life.

Why Read This Book

Would you like your life to be different? Do you find yourself stressed and reactive more than you'd like? If so, then this is the book for you. As you move through these pages, you'll gain the tools to access the reason or reasons you find yourself overreacting and overthinking. Reaction versus Response normalizes what we all experience. As human beings we do our best to support ourselves, our loved ones, families, and communities. When we're constantly reactive it's difficult to cultivate close meaningful relationships and have the lives we desire. We're on the go all the time attempting to live when we're merely surviving. The information provided in this book is designed to help you gain a deeper understanding of yourself, others, and your environment. And the tools shared are practical and easy to implement as they assist you to react less, respond more and experience the beauty of the flow of life.

Tables of Contents

Introduction: 1

Chapter 1 : Why Do We React? 5

Chapter 2 : The Ego 21

Chapter 3 : Intuition 30

Chapter 4 : The Unconscious, Subconscious, and Conscious Mind 40

Chapter 5 : Understanding and Identifying Triggers 50

Chapter 6 : Effects of Trauma 61

Chapter 7 : Facing Fear 71

Chapter 8 : Shame, Blame, and Guilt 79

Chapter 9 : Emotional Intelligence: Wallowing versus Releasing 88

Chapter 10 : You Have to Feel It to Heal It 96

Chapter 11 : Relationships 107

Chapter 12 : Being in the Flow 115

Introduction:

Have you ever reacted in a way that didn't fit the situation? Did it scare you? Or did you feel shame or guilt afterward? Or did you feel justified in your actions? I know I have. Years ago, before I decided to live a healthier life, I constantly reacted to situations in ways that were incongruent with the circumstances. Having a flat tire felt like it was the end of the world. Being late for work meant I was a horrible person. Making a low grade on a test meant I was stupid. I had all these limiting beliefs that ruled my life, and I was highly emotional and reactive. During this time, I was also struggling with addiction and unprocessed trauma.

Over the years, I've learned to regulate my feelings, adjust my thoughts, and shift my beliefs which have helped me reduce my reactions. It's much easier to respond than react, and I move into flow more frequently. I still react and get triggered, but I handle it differently, which is what's important. My journey has been challenging and rewarding.

I've compromised my relationships and watched others do the same as a result of unprocessed trauma, incongruent reactions, addictions, and mental health issues. When we're constantly reacting, it makes it difficult to bond deeply—making long-lasting nurturing connections impossible.

Our connections to ourselves, family, friends, and nature are what make us healthy and strong. If we are lacking in this area, we become weak and more susceptible to outside influences that separate us from each other. That's why doing your inner work is imperative if you want to bring forth your heart's desire.

Reacting is something that happens all the time all over the world. It's neither good nor bad. Reactions provide information, and they let you know what needs your attention.

When I discuss reacting in the book, I mean reacting in a way that's incongruent for the situation—a reaction that doesn't fit the circumstances. I see this all the time with clients, friends, loved ones, and the world. We take things personally, get triggered, and overlap our past with our present—making it difficult to maintain long-lasting bonds and connections.

Over the last eighteen years, I've had the pleasure of helping clients and mentees become more present, reduce their reactions, learn to respond, and move into the flow. Watching change unfold in my life and the lives of others gave me the motivation to write this book. As I share how I've overcome challenges and how others have done the same, my intention is to spark the creative part of you and the healer within. I've also shared tools and techniques that will help you shift the trajectory of your life if that's what you desire.

This information provides ways for you to become more aware of yourself and others and to let go of those things that hold you back. Please edit them when necessary and make them fit into your understanding of yourself and the world. You are the custodian of your body, mind, and spirit, so it's up to you what you want to create for yourself. Remember this as you move through these pages. Take what works, edit it if needed, make it yours, then let go of the rest.

Reaction Versus Response

Huge changes are taking place in our world, so it's time for all of us to do our work and connect. We are stronger together. We are capable of magical things when we release the pain from our past and allow the love to flow through. You are divine as ALL things are. Doing your work shows others they can do the same.

It only takes a small portion of the population to shift its consciousness. According to Gregg Braden, a renowned scientist and teacher, it only takes the square root of 1 percent of the population to change it. That's a small number. So what you do does make a difference. ***Do the work—you're worth it!***

Chapter 1
Why Do We React?

Have you ever flipped someone off in traffic? I know I have. Did you feel justified in the moment? Did they deserve it for cutting you off and almost driving you off the road? When you're put in a situation that threatens your life, fear occurs. Once you realize you're safe and unharmed, typically, anger sets in. Anger vibrates higher than fear. So it's a natural reaction to feel anger as opposed to fear and then express it as rage. After experiencing this repeatedly and continually having the same reaction, the pattern of behavior becomes familiar and hardwired into your system. Now you have a set way to react. Since you have literally downloaded this program into your subconscious, it becomes an automatic reaction. So when someone cuts you off in traffic, your default program may be to flip them off and possibly yell profanities at them. The more you choose this reaction, the deeper it's embedded in your system. Note I said choose. It is a choice. But at the time, it feels as if it's automatic. That's why when you attempt to change your reaction into a response, it's challenging.

Most people will, at some point, realize that it's better for themselves and others not to flip people off in traffic and/or cuss them out. Yet, some will hold their stance and justify their action until the day they die, which is their choice. What if you could minimize your reactions and quickly move into responding and forgiving? Does that sound impossible or doable? You may be fully aware of what triggers you to react, or you may be just starting to realize your triggers. Wherever you're in the learning process, the tools, tips, and techniques provided throughout these pages will teach you ways to reduce reactions and triggers, which will allow space for you to respond and then move into the flow of life. We'll also explore the origin of the reactions and how to heal the wounds that drive them. This will assist you as you release the wounds of the past and integrate the new perceptions of yourself that are supportive and loving.

Personally, I prefer to live my life from a state of peace, joy, and love, and continually flipping people off in traffic and justifying it does not support that lifestyle. Granted, we all slip and have rough days. When I have one of those days, it takes about three to five seconds before I send the offender (in my mind) an apology. I usually say, "I'm sorry, I was wrong. I send you love and light." Becoming more aware of yourself is the key to moving from reacting to your world to responding to it. Understanding how triggers work is also helpful. Again, looking within and observing how you feel and what you're thinking is important. Most of the people I meet are very critical of themselves, which sets the stage for more reaction and less response. When we've internalized a ruthless inner critique from childhood, we struggle with receiving feedback that's in any way considered negative. This is another reason people struggle with change. Many of us have been conditioned to motivate ourselves by using shaming self-talk, which may work in the interim, but eventually falters and becomes toxic to you and the people around you.

The idea is to live the best life we can, which is what I've been taught and choose to do. Being angry, resentful, and apathetic takes much more energy than being happy. Granted, a lot of people have no idea what it's like to experience consistent happiness and joy. If you're one of those people, don't be discouraged. We all must start somewhere. It's learning to embrace yourself no matter how you feel and learning to observe that part of you that's struggling. Most of us will never live 100 percent of our lives in bliss. You're human, and humans feel. Feelings are what connect you with yourself and all things. It's about learning to actually feel your feelings instead of analyzing them.

You may be wondering what qualifications I have that support what I'm sharing with you. First and most importantly, I'm a human being, and I've lived a colorful life filled with pain, fear, love, and light. I've overcome many challenges and heartbreaks with lots of help from loved ones, gifted healers, and counselors. I've chosen the path of living, and I no longer live in a world dominated by survival and victimhood. Logistically, I practice counseling and healing work in private practice in Oklahoma City. I'm a licensed drug and alcohol counselor and mental health counselor. I'm also a certified hypnotherapist and certified emotional freedom technique (EFT) practitioner. Other roles I align with are writer, artist, actor, and mother—the latter being the most important.

I've been blessed with a handsome, gifted son who continues to motivate me to be the best I can be.

Throughout this book I'll refer to feelings as vibrating high or low. This is in reference to a 20-year longitudinal study done by Dr. David Hawkins which he published in his book titled, Power versus Force. He calibrated feelings and emotions from a scale of 0 to 1000. In vibrational order the lower vibrating feelings are as follows; 20 shame, 30 guilt, 50 apathy, 75 grief, 100 fear, 125 desire, 150 anger, 175 pride. The lower vibrating feelings are considered forceful. When you're in these feelings you're attempting to force your way through life. That's why it's more difficult to do daily tasks and to live life to the fullest when you're in these frequencies. The fulcrum point is 200 which is courage where things shift into power. The higher vibrating feelings are: 200 courage, 250 neutrality, 310 willingness, 350 acceptance, 400 reason, 500 love, 540 joy, 600 peace, and enlightenment is from 700-1000. When you're in the high frequencies and living in power things will flow easily to you most of the time because power is a state of abundance. The frequencies are higher so there's no sense of lack. The energy is flowing and free. When you're in forceful feelings or frequencies there's a deficit so you're pulling from yourself and others.

Reaction Versus Response

Remember, feelings aren't good or bad, right, or wrong. They just provide information. When you judge yourself and your feelings you lose the ability to reflect upon them. Meaning, when you judge your behavior then you'll tend to deny your behavior and be unwilling to change. So, do your best to refer to feelings as information. We all move through these frequencies during our lives so it's normal to experience all ranges of feelings and/or frequencies.

Having reactions are a normal part of being human. It's when they become harmful to you, your health, and your relationships that something needs to change. Fear, shame, and guilt are huge driving forces of reactions. The more repressed lower vibrating feelings we have, such as these, the more reactive we are. And parents, employers, families, organizations, and government entities have used fear, shame, and guilt to motivate us to do what they want us to do. Internalizing a perpetrator starts at a young age. The key is to change your relationship with yourself first. Then, how you relate with others will change.

Changing your patterns can be challenging, mostly because you've been doing them for a long time, so they're familiar. Many people give up on change because of the discomfort they feel when they attempt to do things in another way. All change is uncomfortable at first. The issue gets exacerbated when you attempt other ways to control yourself. After many unsuccessful attempts at transformation, most people succumb to defeat and do their best to adapt to the behavior they're struggling with changing.

When you feel continually out of control, your body and mind will stay on "alert" to gain some sense of peace and equilibrium. This is when obsessive-compulsive and addictive behaviors start. This is also when you'll tend to seek solace in activities and relationships. These behaviors are attempts to find a solution to the issue. No one I've ever met likes feeling out of control. The mind and body are designed to seek safety and regulation. So adaptive behaviors are used. Each of us has specific ways that we've learned to suppress, repress, and express what we're experiencing. The problem is the truth needs to be heard, felt, and released. You have an innate understanding within you that knows when you're going against your true nature. Therefore, you feel internal conflict. Again, this internal conflict sets the stage for a reactive life.

Reaction Versus Response

Internal conflict has its own energy. It drives the system to react instead of respond. Also, all of us have experienced some type of trauma at some point in our lives, making the body and mind more sensitive and reactive to the environment. This also fuels the need for more adaptive behaviors. Some common adaptive behaviors include justification, rationalization, and blaming. Our world promotes these, making it more challenging to embrace forgiveness and move into mindful responding and then into flow.

Typically, when I begin working with a client, they're reactionary in nature. They seek assistance to help see the parts of themselves they're unaware of. We all have blind spots. That's why we're all here on earth together. We're here to help each other see the reflections in the other. Reacting limits the way we see ourselves and others. We tend to react from a place of pain or fear. As you learn to move more into responding, it'll be easier for you to see and understand how others reflect things back to you that need your attention. You're welcome to look deeper into the mirrors in relationships by reading my other book, *SO.ARE.YOU*. I go in-depth about how mirrors in relationships help us heal. We'll briefly address the concept in this book.

Most of us are constantly on the move attempting to keep up with work, family, and friends. This lifestyle promotes living a reactionary life. Typically, when I start working with a client, we have to explore ways to reduce their stress which entails scaling back their commitments and attempting to balance their schedule so it's more supportive for their self-care and growth. You have power over your life. You can change your schedule to fit your needs. This is one of the ways to help you move from reacting to responding quickly because when you're overly stressed and have too many things to accomplish, you'll have very little to no energy for yourself.

A client named Sam started counseling to reduce work stress. He'd been working for a company for fifteen years and was experiencing higher levels of stress than before. He stated, "I just need some basic stress management skills, and then I'll be good." As we progressed in counseling, he uncovered childhood trauma that he self-medicated with workaholism. He'd become overly sensitive to stress and struggled to regulate his feelings and thoughts. This was exacerbated by a change in leadership. He'd been under a supportive boss for many years, and the new director micromanaged Sam and didn't value his expertise.

His high-stress work life, coupled with past trauma and unsupportive management, made it difficult for Sam to regulate his feelings and thoughts. When he started counseling, his body and mind were on constant alert, making it difficult for him to respond to his environment. He'd been living this way for many years. So becoming aware that he was reactive was the first step for him in learning to respond to himself and his environment.

It's unfortunate, but Sam's story isn't uncommon. Being busy and productive has been ingrained in most of us since birth. We must work hard to be good contributing members of society. This belief causes a lot of pain for many because it installs a false truth that hard work makes you a good person, and you'll get what you deserve if you're a hard worker. This is incorrect and harmful. I used to subscribe to this belief, and it only caused me pain in the long run. It fuels the reactionary lifestyle that'll only deteriorate your body, mind, and spirit. It can only be maintained for a brief period before it collapses and begins to break down all areas of your life.

Since we're living in a world of constant reaction, it's easy to justify your position and admit no responsibility. Prior to hitting bottom and admitting defeat, justification is the common pathway. To maintain this, you must justify your behavior. I've met many people who refuse to take responsibility for their behavior. They'd rather die than admit that they're wrong or have contributed to the pain and struggle in their life. This is usually connected to repressed pain from the past. If you find stillness, your repressed feelings will surface. The key is learning to sit with it and allow it to flow out and through you. At that point, the core memories, beliefs, and thoughts can surface. Then you can release the past. **You must feel it to heal it.**

Many years ago, I too held the stance of victimhood. I felt justified because I'd been victimized during childhood and adulthood. The shame and guilt would surface, and I'd quickly repress them and continue justifying my actions. Does any of this sound familiar? I had to embrace the pain and seek help to process my past and forgive myself and others. Then, I was able to live a full life. The idea is not to deny being victimized but to sit with yourself and allow the feelings to surface and release them so you can honor the part of you that was wounded. This allows you to let it all go and move into the flow of life and experience love and joy.

Reaction Versus Response

Have you ever justified your reaction and realized later it was unfounded? I can say with confidence that most of us on the planet have done this at some point in our lives. When you justify your behavior, there's a part of you that realizes that the situation could have been dealt with differently. If you're confident in how you handled things, then there's no reason to justify it. There's a sense of calmness and confidence that assures you that you made the appropriate choice for yourself in the moment.

Learning to override your need to be right is a process of moving from reaction to response to flow. Our world is designed to keep us busy and engaged in external activities. So by design, it ignites the flight, fight, freeze and fawn reactions in the brain. When this continues to happen over and over again, you become programmed to react instead of responding to your world, which makes it impossible to connect to your natural flow of energy. Learning to pause, assess, and then respond is the first step to overriding the need to be right. You must learn to pause to determine why you feel justified in your reaction. Then, you can access what is underneath it, meaning what memory or experience was triggered. I'll outline the process more in-depth throughout this book.

It's generally best to walk away or take a breath and pause before reengaging in a situation where you've reacted and are demanding that you're right. There's always evidence to prove any point that any human has brought forth. So, learning to honor that in yourself will help you honor that in another person. You'll never find a solid solution if you continue to hold your stance with anger and resentment. As Einstein said, **"You cannot solve a problem from the same consciousness that created it."** You'll not solve your problem from a reactionary state. The feelings that drive reactions are lower vibrating, such as shame, grief, apathy, fear, and anger. When you're in these states, you cannot experience pure empathy.

Throughout this book, I'm going to use the terms reaction, response, and flow. A reaction by itself is not an unhealthy thing. It's how your body, mind, and spirit react to something that has occurred within you, possibly because of something that took place outside of you. That can also happen in reverse. For example, you think, *I look horrible*, then you retreat inside yourself, and your body language expresses that belief by hanging your head down, rounding your shoulders, and having a sad expression on your face. What you're reacting to happened outside of you, but the reaction happened within.

A response is a mindful way to interact with yourself and others in your world. Using the earlier example, you have the same thought *I look horrible*. Instead of allowing your body to react to your thought, you respond to it by taking a deep breath and respond to yourself by releasing any feelings and changing your inner self-talk. As you're moving from reacting to responding, you'll become more efficient at this. The goal is to move into the flow of life. This is where you trust yourself, and then loving responses occur without the need to pause or think—they just become natural.

Moving into flow is the goal. Yet, remember you're human, so you'll slip at times and react. Understanding how draining reacting is and how it affects you and others is important. Reactions such as screaming at someone for accidentally bumping into you at the grocery store are heavy and draining. Even visual reactions send heavy energy to others. They don't have to be outbursts to affect you and others. These are types of reactions that occur regularly all around the world with all kinds of people in different types of situations.

Some people can regulate their feelings and thoughts more easily than others and react less. There are many different factors that come into play in our world today; high levels of trauma, post-traumatic stress disorder, depression, anxiety, homelessness, intense stress, socioeconomic status, the political climate, and our health issues and structures, to name a few. The playing field most of us have initially created for ourselves doesn't support moving into the flow. Yet herein lies the challenge for us all, which is to go within and create a new paradigm—one that supports and embraces the natural flow of life. We ALL have what it takes to live the life of our dreams—one filled with color and contrast.

In the next chapter, we'll explore the relationship between the ego and intuition.

Chapter 1 Questions:

1. Think about how you react, respond, and move into flow.

2. Write about question #1.

3. Write about a reaction you had where you justified your position and later realized you were wrong.

4. Expand on this experience and how you dealt with it inside yourself and if you took actions during and or afterward.

Chapter 2
The Ego

What exactly is the ego? Most people think the ego is a negative aspect of your personality and think of it as a sign of arrogance or an overinflated sense of self. I used to think this too. Do you? Throughout my journey, I've heard several different definitions that are more inclusive and loving. The first was from Anita Moorjani's book titled *What If This Is Heaven?* She discusses how the ego helps us know the boundaries between each other, meaning I know where you begin and I end. I'd heard this saying years ago in recovery groups for codependency as well, and when I read her book, it became clearer to me. It opened me up to understanding that the ego is not a "bad" thing. Granted, it can get imbalanced, as she discusses in her book. For example, a client named Judith started therapy to work through addiction issues and codependency. The most challenging relationship she had was with her mother. Judith felt that any decision she made, she had to consult her mother first. She said, "I know I need to stop asking her and telling her things, but I feel guilty if I don't. I'm so afraid of upsetting her. I know I'm looking for her approval." As Judith worked through her guilt, she was able to stand firmly within herself, tolerate her feelings, and make choices despite her mother disagreeing. Prior to her increased awareness of herself and her patterns, her ego was imbalanced, and she wasn't following her higher awareness. She was operating from old beliefs and memories that told her that to stay safe, she must compromise herself and sacrifice her wants and needs. Here her ego overrode her intuition. The ego was in control of her thoughts, feelings, and actions. She was reactionary and struggled with responding from her new understandings and ideas. As she moved through balancing herself, she learned to assess what were others' issues and what were her own, hence knowing where others ended and where she began.

The other concept of the ego was shared with me by a trusted healer I've consulted for several years,

Dr. Gary Cone. He said, "The ego's job is to collect information from the past and bring it to you in the present for assessment." This also resonated with me. For example, if you have an experience now and it reminds you of an experience you had in the past, the ego brings the information from the past to the present. Then you have an overlap. I see clients do this regularly. Their reaction to situations happening in the present moment is layered with feelings, thoughts, and beliefs from the past. This creates a reaction instead of a response until you learn to pause and assess the trigger. We'll explore this later in the book. An imbalanced ego will keep you in a reactionary state, and you'll loop in lower vibrating feelings such as anger, fear, shame, and guilt. This reduces your ability to have empathy for yourself and others, creating separation and disconnection.

This applied to Judith as well. She was lost in the past and allowed her ego to run the show. All she really wanted was love from her mother and to feel love for her mother. She was also unable in the beginning to see herself separate from her mother. Her thoughts and feelings were entangled with her mother's. As she learned to separate herself with internal and external boundaries, it became easier for her to respond to her mother and live her own life.

The ego also fears death and tends to believe you're attempting to kill it. So, it starts concocting scenarios to hold its stance and maintain the behavior pattern that you're attempting to change. When you act out behaviors repeatedly, they become familiar, and familiarity tends to represent comfort, even when the behaviors are destructive and uncomfortable. Most of us are looking for ways to soothe and avoid any type of pain or discomfort. The problem is avoiding the pain causes more pain. Then we seek outside ourselves for solutions and end up in a never-ending loop of dis-ease with a deep-seated feeling of hopelessness.

The ego is not something to discard. It's something to embrace and guide. As discussed, many teachings paint it as a bad thing that needs to be destroyed. When you think this way, it'll defend itself, and an internal battle is destined to occur. Internal war will create external war. Do you relate? I know I do. I've experienced internal war many times throughout my journey. It's a natural part of being human. So do your best not to judge yourself or think you're doing something wrong because you're having internal battles. Again, it's normal to struggle and doubt. It's about learning to move into the flow of life and allow the beautiful energy within you and around you to guide you to bliss. Yes, bliss. It's possible for all of us to experience bliss. It may not be every minute of every day, but it is possible. If you've experienced it in your life, bravo! You know it exists, so you can access it again. Not to worry if you have not. You will if it is something you desire.

As you move through these chapters and begin implementing new ideas and concepts, you're changing your brain, heart, and entire system. Bringing in new ideas shakes your bubble and expands your consciousness; at times, you'll be uncomfortable. I invite you to embrace the discomfort and remind yourself this is part of the process.

Take a moment and think of something you do well that you learned either growing up or as an adult. For example, riding a bike, playing an instrument, writing a poem, or starting a new job. Then take yourself back to the moment before you mastered it, maybe the first time you rode your bike or the first day of a new job. Pause for a moment and take a deep breath and allow yourself to remember and experience the feelings and thoughts as if you're there now. What are you feeling? Discomfort, fear, excitement? Contemplate this. Take a big breath and bring yourself back into the moment and assess how you feel and think about things now. Is it easy for you to ride a bike? Did you master that job? Most likely, you feel and think completely differently than you did when you started.

When I was sixteen years old, I started martial arts. It was difficult, and I got angry because I was uncoordinated and clumsy. I'd never experienced this before; sports had always come easy to me, and this was hard. It was a big lesson in perseverance and patience. One of the coaches took me aside and worked with me individually, and eventually, it became a part of me, and I excelled at it. Sometimes introducing new behaviors or skills is easy, and other times it's difficult. Embrace both. If something is hard, then channel the frustration into your practice, and know it'll get easier if you stick with it.

My experience with martial arts is also an example of ego running wild. I was expecting to be an expert at Taekwondo immediately, and when that didn't happen, I was angry and frustrated. I had an expectation of what I would experience based on my past experiences. Since I wasn't in the moment,

I wasn't teachable. I had to hit a breaking point before I was able to receive instruction and allow myself to be a novice. My imbalanced ego fed me reasons to feel superior initially and then inferior later, and neither helped me flow. Also, the lower vibrating feelings I was experiencing sent me into an activated state which made it difficult to access the parts of me that were teachable at the time. This still happens today, but it's less frequent. Now I know to pause, take a breath, and move into flow, where I allow myself to follow the energy. It's not about being perfect. It's about learning to let go faster and honor each moment, whether it's uncomfortable or blissful.

What most of us have done is listened to our ego and squashed our intuition. So decisions are made based on old programming, which include what parents, peers, organizations, and institutions have imposed upon us. The ego has gotten so loud that it overshadows the inner voice for most of us. This is another factor that feeds the reactionary lifestyle. Since most of us tend to ignore our inner voice and go with the ego mind, we then create a self-fulfilling prophecy, meaning we draw to us what we focus on. This can be positive or negative depending on what's running in your subconscious and unconscious mind. The goal is to change unsupportive belief patterns to supportive ones. Then, once you've mastered the supportive belief patterns and they're ingrained in your subconscious, you get to move into the natural flow of life.

Life flows in a more loving manner when the ego serves your higher consciousness. This requires discipline, which means to teach. You must teach your ego to not override your intuition. Remember, it's a process of evolution and growth that each of us must go through at our own pace. I've learned over the years that I can't force growth and expansion. It comes when it comes. Yet, continuing to experience new things and create more space for change makes transformation more tolerable and, at times, enjoyable. Do your best to be patient with yourself. Life is a journey of wonder and exploration. If it's difficult for you to see and understand life this way, that's okay. You **CAN** always change your mind!

Chapter 2 Questions:

1. Write down your definition of your ego.

2. Then, write down a new way to look at the ego using the principles described in Chapter 2.

3. Write down an experience where your ego was imbalanced.

4. Expand on how you felt and what you thought during this experience.

Chapter 3
Intuition

What is intuition? I usually hear people refer to it as a "gut feeling" or a "knowing" that something is right or wrong. Others may call it a premonition about an event that's going to occur. We all have the ability to attune to our intuition and/or knowing. My experiences have taught me that the more aware I am of myself and the more quiet my thinking becomes, the easier it is to receive intuitive information. This takes commitment and awareness of yourself. Some people are born with a more heightened intuition than others. Yet these people must continue to clear their traumas like anyone else to clearly receive the messages from their intuition. Most importantly, it's about trusting yourself and listening to your inner voice. Some people may refer to it as God.

Others may refer to it as Spirit, the universe, a higher self, or a higher power. It's your internal guidance system. Even though many people think of this energy as outside themselves, it occurs within and is projected outward. When you know something, you experience the knowing within yourself then it is affirmed and/or created externally. Basically, you receive validation in the external world. We'll explore this further later in the book.

Understanding your intuition is an important part of learning how to move into the flow of life. When you trust yourself, it becomes natural to follow your heart which leads to a fulfilling life of contrast and wonder. Have you ever felt a nudge to do something, and you listened, and it was a benefit to you? I can confidently say most people would say "Yes." What did you feel when this occurred? I know I've felt validated and excited that I followed my guidance. How about you? What about when you didn't follow this guidance? How did you feel? What did you think? Were you frustrated with yourself, or were you gentle? I hope you were gentle, but most of us tend to lean toward the ruthless inner critique that thinks criticism is motivating. Sound familiar? Negative self-talk is something that inhibits flow, activates an imbalanced ego, and shuts down intuition. As you continue to release your old ideas of yourself and embrace new ones, negative self-talk will be minimal if you desire it to be.

The idea that motivation is best done with shaming words and actions is something from your past. You may have had a critical parent or caregiver and a loving, understanding grandparent. Having both is helpful when letting go of the negative beliefs because you have a reference that there are understanding and loving people in the world. When you walk through change, it's more difficult when you haven't had an understanding person to reference. It's virtually impossible to shield someone from the critical aspects of the world. So, no matter what your experiences have been, learning to release negative beliefs and adopt positive ones is important.

I was at one of my son's T-ball games when he was five years old, and one of his teammates, Wallace, walked onto the field without his hat. His mother started screaming at him, "Get your fucking hat! What are you thinking? Get it now!" It took everything I had not to confront this woman. I was so angry and conflicted about what to do. I decided to walk away after I saw she was not going to do it again. I also needed to breathe through the intense anger I was feeling. I was shocked at how this woman treated her son. The intense anger I was feeling inhibited me from responding to her, so my best option was to walk away.

If this situation had happened earlier in my life, the outcome would've been much different. I would most likely have confronted her with intense anger, and we possibly would've had a physical altercation. I would've made things much worse and justified my actions. Before I started my journey of healing and expansion, I lived a life full of justified reactions. Because of the environment I was raised in, I had to be alert all the time. There was addiction, neglect, and abusive behavior from early childhood through high school. This conditioned me to be highly aware of my surroundings and other people and their feelings. This state is continually referred to as hypervigilance. Since I was hyperaware and intuitive, I learned to believe everything I thought and felt. This became a big problem for me, especially in relationships, because, as discussed earlier, my ego would bring back information from my past and overlap it onto my current situation. I would stand firm in my reactions that were incorrect. I was unable to pause and see the connections and have different discussions.

After moving out on my own, my addictions became more intense, and my relationships more abusive. This clouded my judgment and muddied my intuition even more. It took years of healing within and seeking guidance from trusted mentors and counselors to understand who I am. Learning who you are is imperative to clearing your past and being more in the flow of life. This is another topic discussed in my book *SO.ARE.YOU*. Ask yourself the question, "Who am I?" Explore what comes up for you. Know the answer will change as you grow and expand. It seems basic, but it can elicit many thoughts, feelings, and memories that will help you uncover more of your truth.

Wallace's mother used shame and anger to motivate him. What may have been installed was, "I must be perfect, or my mother will scream at me and/or I'll be embarrassed in front of my teammates." From this one event, he learned that anger and shame are motivators. Now, he may not use the same type of delivery his mother used, but he'll have an inhibiting negative interpretation of himself and women because of his experience, especially since this was most likely not the first time she'd done this. Negative thought patterns may motivate you briefly but will eventually fail you because they create negative feelings about who you are. They keep you from connecting to your higher self and listening to your intuition.

As soon as Wallace's mother saw him without his hat, she immediately reacted by screaming at him. There was little to no time for conscious thought. Her reaction had to have come from her past experiences and her view of herself. There was justification in her verbal and physical communication. Typically, when this type of behavior happens in public, most of us feel shame and/or guilt. Now, we may not acknowledge these feelings at the time they occur because they're so uncomfortable to sit with. We usually move to anger because it's a higher vibrating feeling. It's unlikely Wallace's mother apologized to him for her behavior. If his mother did take responsibility for her behavior and addressed what was at the core of her reaction, then she'd be able to respond to her son in a loving way. But if she repressed her feelings and chose not to assess herself, then she'd continue to react to her son and her environment in a similar way. This is called being emotionally unintelligent and unaware of how one affects others. This is a great example of why it's important to know yourself and explore your thoughts, feelings, and beliefs. When you can own your behavior and make amends, it makes it easier to connect with your loved ones and enjoy life.

After I released the anger I felt toward Wallace's mother, I was able to break down the situation and understand what occurred. The intense feelings and emotions made it difficult to feel pure empathy for her. This is normal for all of us. When we're experiencing lower vibrating feelings that activate our brains to fight, flee, fawn, or freeze, we're not capable of feeling compassion and empathy as we can when we're experiencing higher vibrating feelings such as courage, willingness, and love. In the moment, some of my thoughts were, *Who the hell do you think you are? And how dare you speak to him that way? You need help.* There were many others that were more aggressive and angrier. I wanted to intervene and protect Wallace and tell his mother how horrible she was being to her son. It wasn't my place to tell this woman how to parent her son, even though part of me wanted to set her straight.

She was most likely parented in the same way, so it was normal for her to behave like this. Also, the feelings I experienced were mine and based upon my belief system and how I see the world. The difference is I have learned to regulate my feelings and not emote them most of the time. Hence, I walked off, took deep breaths, and processed it with a family member. It took a while for me to let it go because of the empathy I had for Wallace and the justified anger I felt for his mother. My ego wanted a confrontation, and my intuition or higher self knew to move on. The work I'd done over the years paid off, and it continues to.

None of us are perfect. We all fall short at times. I have and will continue to have shortcomings. You will too. It's how you recover that's important. We have feelings, thoughts, and beliefs that shape who we are and how we behave. Until we explore these, we'll continue to react to our world in the same way we always have. We're all faced with challenges and understanding why you react to certain situations is helpful when learning to flow with life. We all react, respond, and flow with our environment. But most of us do it unconsciously. As you learn more about yourself and clear the backlogged pain from your past, you'll move into the flow of life and begin consciously creating your world. We all have this ability. We do it every day. We tend to believe our experiences are out of our control when we're co-creators of our reality. It takes commitment to release those things that inhibit you from believing you're a powerful creator. It doesn't typically happen overnight, so be patient with yourself. We're all on our own timetable. Yes, it is challenging, but I promise you it is worth it!

Chapter 3 Questions:

1. Write down a time you followed your intuition and how it helped the situation.

2. Write down a time you ignored your intuition. What was the outcome?

3. Have you ever acted in a similar way to Wallace's mom? If so, write about it and how you felt and thought then and how you feel and think about it now. Have you forgiven yourself?

4. Write down anything that blocks you from trusting your intuition. Beliefs, experiences etc.

5. Explore and discuss ways that help you trust your intuition.

Chapter 4
The Unconscious, Subconscious, and Conscious Mind

Sigmund Freud broke the mind into three parts: the conscious, the subconscious, and the preconscious. He compared these parts to an iceberg and how the part we see above water is the conscious mind which is only a small portion of the mind. The subconscious is the part directly under the water that you may be able to see slightly, and the unconscious is the part deep down that's not visible. For most people, the majority of the aspects of the self reside in the latter two. The parts underneath are comprised of roughly 90 percent of your memories and beliefs. The other 10 percent is what lies in your conscious mind.

It's helpful to use this model to understand why you react to certain things in specific ways. The unconscious and subconscious contain an accumulation of your beliefs, thoughts, feelings, and memories. The subconscious mind is accessible to you when you slow down and pay attention to what's occurring within you. You're able to bring forth things from the subconscious to the conscious mind, typically with minimal effort. The unconscious mind is not readily accessible because it takes increased awareness and healing to bring forth the information it holds. This is the part where beliefs, experiences, and traumas are stored. According to Freud, it's possible to have glimpses of this information through your dreams and clues within language patterns. I've experienced this and also witnessed it with clients. There are also expressions and behaviors that give clues to what's going on beneath the surface in each of us.

What lies beneath the surface is similar to the programs or apps running in the background of your computer or phone. They're constantly running and affect how the computer operates.

As you expand your understanding of yourself and your subconscious and unconscious patterns, it'll become easier to regulate your feelings, thoughts, and emotions, which aids in responding and moving into the flow of life.

For example, have you ever driven home and not remembered driving there? That's because you've driven that route so many times you don't need to be consciously aware to make it home. You've mastered the skill, so your subconscious mind took over and drove the car better than you would if you were thinking about how to drive and where to go. This is another reason to become aware of the beliefs that are in your subconscious and unconscious mind because some are helpful, and some are not. The goal is to bring as much information from the other aspects of the mind into the conscious mind to increase your awareness of yourself and your ability to regulate your feelings, thoughts, and actions.

Roger came to see me to improve his ability to manage stress. After a few sessions, it was clear he had deeper struggles that needed attention. He'd experienced intense childhood abuse and neglect. After Roger accepted there were more pieces to his puzzle, he started processing his trauma. He struggled with negative self-talk, blocking beliefs, emotional dysregulation, and physical health challenges. One day he was sitting in my office waiting for me to return from the kitchen. During this time, a young child who was with a colleague's client ran into the office and sat next to him.

When I returned, he said, "A little girl came in and made herself comfortable right here next to me. She spoke to me for a bit and then ran off to her mom."

I immediately got excited, and thought, *This is a perfect affirmation moment*, and I said, "How did you feel after that?"

"I love kids, and they love me."

I went a step further and said, "See, you have good energy. That doesn't happen to everyone."

He said, "Well, I used to think that until they did what they did." He was referring to being written up at work for something he said wasn't accurate.

I paused a moment and challenged him. "So, you're telling me you're going to believe what they said and not what just happened here in this office?"

"Well," he said, slightly shaken, "they said I was horrible."

"So, are you going to believe them or what you just experienced?" I asked. He pondered for a while and continued to struggle with the two narratives floating through his mind.

The next day he texted me, "Children and animals do love me."

This is a classic example of how the subconscious and unconscious minds operate. Roger had been clearing old patterns for several years at this point and was in the process of accepting the severity of his childhood trauma. Since he hadn't fully processed, accepted, and released it, he was more susceptible to aligning with the negative narrative he'd downloaded during childhood: that he was defective and bad. During the session, he challenged me that he wasn't loveable or likable because of his past and recent work experience. Even though his trauma was at the forefront of his mind, there were still positive experiences that he could draw from to shift his narrative.

Have you ever argued with someone about being a bad person or attempted to convince them you were wrong? It's interesting how so many people will stand firm in a negative belief that elicits shame and guilt. As discussed, this is because negative beliefs have energy, and most of them have been running in your subconscious and unconscious mind for a long time which tends to make it difficult to change them. Also, there's a payoff for every behavior. For Roger, his payoff was he could hide in the corner and not be seen. As a child, being seen meant possible and unpredictable danger.

He also reversed the blame onto himself so he could maintain a bond with his caregivers. If he blamed them, he couldn't consciously stay in the household. In that context, it was important for him to think he was bad. His childhood memories impeded his success yet protected him from his horrific memories, hence creating internal conflict. That's why he reverted to the old belief that he was bad and struggled accepting the truth about how the little girl was drawn to him. The work he'd been doing had unearthed some of his unconscious beliefs, and they'd move in and out of his conscious and subconscious mind.

The subconscious mind holds the keys to our success and failure. As discussed with Roger, the core beliefs are downloaded during childhood and then reinforced throughout your life. New beliefs are possible through conditioning, repetition, and integration. Your experiences with family, friends, work connections, and media affect your belief system and how you see yourself and the world. That's why the saying "hang with the winners" has truth. You're influenced by your core connections, whether you like it or not. Changing those connections is one way to change how you view yourself and others.

The first step to changing beliefs is to become aware of them. That's why it's helpful to have a trusted counselor, mentor, support group, friend, or family member who'll be honest with you about your behavior. It's much easier to receive feedback from someone you love and respect. Shame and guilt tend to surface during confrontation, and that's why learning to honor, embrace, and release your feelings is important. This helps you embody humility and hear what another is sharing with you and assess if it's something you need to address or not. Sometimes we project our issues onto others, and they do the same to us. So learning to assess within yourself will help you take in what needs your attention and release what does not. Another way to look at someone you respect and love giving you feedback is they're **carefronting** you. They're carefully and lovingly confronting you.

One of my undergrad teachers used this word consistently during group counseling class. It changed the meaning of the word for me, and I hope it does for you too. It's a much softer way to give and receive feedback from others. If you practice this way of thinking and relating to others and share it with them, then they can practice with you and share with others.

If any of what's been discussed is foreign to you, don't worry. Your understanding and awareness will increase as you move through the chapters of this book. Some things come quickly, and some take more time. We're all on our own timetable. You'll get frustrated at yourself or others as you move through the process. This is normal. We all struggle and resist transformation because we're hardwired to maintain patterns. That's why most people thrive with routines. There's a sense of safety in them even if they're not supporting wellness. They're familiar and reside in the subconscious. You can do them in your sleep. You don't have to think about what to do next. You're on autopilot, and there's no challenge.

Are you ready for a challenge? I hope you said "Yes!" If you didn't, that's okay too. You'll get there! Anything worth doing is typically uncomfortable in the beginning, especially when dealing with change. Be patient with yourself and keep going. Understanding yourself provides you with the keys to your own kingdom. No one else will ever have access to or the ability to use those keys but you. Why not go for it and figure out what, where, and who those keys are? Remember, it may be rough at times, but that's normal as you move through embracing all aspects of yourself.

I promise you it's worth every uncomfortable memory and every tear you may shed to experience the joy and bliss waiting for you on the other side. Remember, contrast creates rich experiences.

Chapter 4 Review Questions:

1. Write down three negative beliefs that have defined you.

2. Journal about how they have affected your choices.

3. Make a list of beliefs you would like to change.

4. Make a list of beliefs that still serve you and others in a loving way.

5. Have you ever intentionally changed a core belief? If so, write about your process.

Chapter 5
Understanding and Identifying Triggers

When exploring why you react, it's important to differentiate between a trigger and a reaction. A trigger is when you have a reaction to something in your present environment that reminds you of a past event. The thoughts and feelings from the past event are transposed onto the current event. The trigger can be as simple as a smell, word, tone of voice, or facial expression. When you're triggered, your reaction is incongruent with the situation. Basically, you overreact. Many abuse situations are a result of a triggered person or persons. Also, people who struggle with addictions experience triggers that drive them to drink or use drugs despite the adverse consequences.

A simple reaction is reacting to an internal or external stimulus in the present moment, which is congruent with the situation. For example, your friend hides behind a tree, jumps out, and scares you. You scream and possibly attempt to fight them, or you, fawn, freeze or flee. This is a natural reaction to this situation for most of us. If you have had multiple situations like this and possibly have been harmed, you'd also be triggered. But in this situation, most people will immediately react to the person jumping out unexpectedly.

As discussed in previous chapters, learning about how you store and access information helps you understand how your triggers were downloaded into your system. I had a friend say, "If I don't understand how it works, you've lost me." Most of us think this way. We need to intellectually understand how something works before we can grasp the concept and begin implementing it into our lives.

You can address triggers backward or forward, meaning you can understand how your mind works and then grasp your triggers, or you can explore your triggers to understand your mind. This concept is called "the law of reversibility," coined by Neville Goddard. Basically, everything is connected, and you can learn whatever way works best for you. As you continue to explore yourself using the tools and information provided in these pages, allow yourself the space to be a novice and practice the tools the best way that serves you. Sometimes, you may need to put it down for a while and then pick it back up and start again. When it's the right time, you'll know.

A few months ago, I was reading a book and the author made a statement that was triggering for me, and I felt irritated and angry. I put the book down and refused to do his forty-day program. I'd lost respect for him based on something he wrote about his experience that I didn't agree with. I discussed it with my mother, who'd read another book of his, and she added some information that helped me see his point of view differently. After assessing the trigger internally and seeing what it was connected to, the irritation left. My intuition nudged me to go ahead and implement his program, and I love it! It's helped me so much. This is a great example of how a trigger will affect your point of view and keep you looping in the past if not addressed, explored, and released. After I released the energy from the past that was blocking me from moving forward, things flowed, and it was the perfect time to implement the program.

Triggers, at times, are viewed as negative because they're considered the cause of harmful behavior or what initiates it. Actually, they're helpful because they let you know what needs your attention. A lot of treatment focuses on identifying and reducing triggers or avoiding them, especially for people with addictions which is understandable and can be helpful. Yet it's best if you learn to sit with them and release the energy behind them. As discussed, a trigger is an overly intense reaction to an event.

So feelings, thoughts, and emotions are amplified, making the situation seem much bigger than it is. Therefore, it's important to learn to sit with your feelings and release them. If you struggle with substance abuse or addiction and you get triggered, you might drink or use to soothe yourself. This is another reason to explore them and release the charge behind them. Otherwise, you'll never be able to stay sober if that's your goal because you'll be triggered by all the media advertisements and billboards driving down the road. The goal is freedom from any type of bondage, which takes awareness, implementation, and commitment.

Most people are afraid to experience their feelings fully. I've heard so many times, "I'm afraid I'll get stuck in them, and I'll never get out." Or "I'm weak if I cry or show emotions." These are unsupportive beliefs that won't help you reach your goals. They keep you stuck, looping in your mind, and attached to limiting belief patterns. The charge of the feelings, along with the memory tied to them, causes the information from both to be hardwired into your memory. This is how a trigger is created. Even physical traumas are hardwired with the psychological aspect of the event in the body. So physical pain can be a trigger as well. Understanding your triggers can help you understand more of what's lurking in your subconscious and unconscious mind.

Processing your past traumas and identifying your triggers makes walking through conflicts with a friend, family member, or loved one much easier. Your conflict resolution skills become more refined, and you're able to pause and implement them when you know yourself better and how you're wired. Triggers are associated with past events, typically traumatic ones that have an intense energetic charge and are tied to beliefs. It's possible to be aware you're triggered and move through it without acting things out. As you continue to practice your new skills and make them a part of your life, it'll be possible.

The channels that connect you to your past become clear, meaning you become aware of your triggers and reduce them. Some are gone forever, and some you'll continue to work through until you're done with them.

Past clients, Samantha and Abbey, mother and daughter who both struggled with trauma and addiction, had an experience that depicts this beautifully. They were very supportive of each other, and their lives were deeply intertwined. Samantha was receiving a lump sum after refinancing her house and had decided to pay off some of her daughter's debt. The condition was Abbey would pay half of the loan payment. She was excited and surprised by this gesture. The process had gone by quickly and they hadn't discussed things in detail. One morning Abbey woke up and realized that she needed to discuss the terms of the loan because she was feeling uncomfortable with what they agreed too. She was receiving a quarter of the money her mother was borrowing, so she wondered why she was paying half the payment.

Abbey said, "I'd been feeling heavy and irritable since the situation started, and I woke up one morning and realized I'd stuffed my feelings because I was afraid. After I realized this, I felt relief, so I knew I had to talk to my mom."

Abbey called her mother, shared her concerns with her, and stated, "I knew I just needed to talk to you about this because we hadn't had a lengthy discussion about it."

Immediately, Samantha got triggered and went into lockdown mode. She said, "Well, I don't have to give you any money."

This statement triggered Abbey, who then got angry and yelled at Samantha, "See, this is why I didn't want to tell you. All I wanted was to talk about it. There's nothing wrong with that."

This led to intense arguing, which ended in Abbey hanging up on Samantha. After they both released their anger, they were able to discuss how they were triggered and misunderstood each other and were unable to deal with the current situation calmly.

Samantha said, "I got triggered. I was so angry I completely locked down. I couldn't see things clearly. I immediately went to my father, changing the rules on things, especially with money."

Abbey stated, "I got triggered because you didn't listen to what I said and why I said it. So I got angry and yelled."

Afterward, they both apologized and moved past their fears which helped them gain more trust for each other and themselves.

Since both Samantha and Abbey had committed to improving themselves and their relationship and communicating their truths with each other, they were able to move through a tough situation. As you can see, it wasn't without intense feelings, emotions, angry words, and actions. People argue and get angry at times. There's nothing wrong with that. It's how you use the situation to grow and move into forgiveness that's important. It's about the progress that's made in the relationship. Samantha and Abbey struggled for years to communicate and work through conflict. They'd get triggered, shut down, and blame each other for their problems. At times it took weeks for them to slightly resolve situations, and most of them were only partially resolved. After years of releasing the past and learning about themselves, their triggers, and ways to release the pain from their past, they were able to trust each other.

Reaction Versus Response

Both Samantha and Abbey had experienced a lot of traumas during their childhoods and as adults, which caused them to bond in their trauma. Even though they always made it back to each other during conflicts, they never felt completely safe in their relationship until they did the work and forgave each other, the people who had harmed them, and themselves. At this point, they'd formed a new bond, and they both knew within their hearts that neither would leave the other. They were committed to the relationship and supported each other. Their triggers became givers of truth and provided them with the keys to freedom and love.

Understanding where your triggers originate and the reason you react to them is imperative when walking through the change process and creating the life you desire. Your relationships provide the information you need to understand yourself and how you relate to the world. If you feel disconnected from yourself, then you'll feel disconnected from others. One main issue I've heard about in my years of service is people feeling alone and misunderstood. One client stated, "I feel like I'm on an island all alone." If you decide not to deal with your past and learn about your triggers, you'll die unfulfilled and lonely.

We're not here to suffer alone. We're here to embrace our suffering and transmute it into love and joy. That process is much easier to attain with other loving souls. That's why attending self-help groups or going to a trusted counselor or healer is beneficial. When you continually react to your world, it's difficult to trust yourself or others, which makes relationships painful and unfulfilling. If this is where you are, please know you can change, and you can connect and trust. It'll take perseverance and commitment. I've witnessed some amazing transformations in my life, mine included. So that means you can do it too. Remember to keep moving forward and don't ever give up!!

Chapter 5 Questions:

1. Identify a time you were triggered that caused problems in a relationship. Write about how you felt and what you thought.

2. Write about a time you observed someone who was triggered. Did they trigger you too, or were you able to hold space for them? If you've had both experiences journal about them.

3. When you get triggered, what do you notice happens in your body? Write about what you experienced, body sensations, feelings, thoughts etc.

4. Review your answers to these questions and notice if there's any underlined beliefs you notice. Write about what you discovered.

Chapter 6
Effects of Trauma

Trauma can be any type of physical, emotional, or mental disturbance. It doesn't have to be a huge event to cause a trauma response. It all depends on your culture, societal view, and how you process the situation, as well as understand yourself and others. Some traumas are more intense than others, and some are an accumulation of small traumas that create a larger issue.

I attended trauma-informed training, and a colleague discussed her experience with children from a third-world country. She shared that they walked several miles to work at a factory and then back home each day. This was normal and not considered traumatic in their country. In the United States, that would be considered child abuse.

She stated, "I'd ask them how their walk was that day. It was not something out of the ordinary for them at all. Some even enjoyed their walks." Listening to her share her experience reminded me of how experiences are relative to the individual and to listen closely to how people view their experiences. Sometimes if one person views something as horrible and projects their view onto the situation, it can elicit a traumatic reaction in the other. If she'd done this in the situation with the children, it could possibly have traumatized the child. Instead, she mindfully observed and supported the children.

Trauma can also go unrecognized due to minimization by the individual or a helping professional. Pamela struggled with this for years during her treatment for post-traumatic stress disorder. She'd experienced neglect and severe abuse from a young age. She'd been kicked out of her house at the age of fourteen and was sent to live alone in a home that her parents owned. When she started therapy, she was struggling with dark thoughts about harming her loved one and herself.

When she started treatment, she said, "I left when I was fourteen and decided to live on my own at our other house."

After several years of therapy, her dark thoughts cleared, and she was able to see the event for what it was. She stated, "They did kick me out. I didn't want to leave."

Over several years, I had to continually correct her when she'd discuss the event because of how she'd stored it in her memory. It was safer for her to blame herself in order to stay bonded with her parents. Storing this incorrectly was one of the reasons she was having internal battles. In this situation, it was important to continually challenge her beliefs because to heal deep trauma, **you have to see it for what it is, so you can feel it and release it**. Otherwise, you repress it, and it becomes much larger than it is. The internal battle becomes one of repression instead of release. It never heals this way. It just stays buried under the surface, causing mental, emotional, and physical disturbances.

When you live in an environment like Pamela's, where you're constantly experiencing trauma, your system automatically pushes the feelings, thoughts, and beliefs aside for later processing. This happens because it's not safe to process what you're experiencing in the moment. This is why Pamela's trauma didn't begin to cause major disruptions until after she had been sober for over five years and was in a stable relationship. She had to reach a level of safety and calmness for things to begin to surface. Trauma also surfaces intermittently for many people. The memories break through and are then immediately repressed with some other behavior. That's why trauma is a primary driver of addiction and mental health issues.

Unlike wild animals, humans attempt to hide from their trauma and prolong its release. The chemicals that are dumped in the body during a traumatic event are designed to prepare you to move out of a dangerous situation and then to safety. Once you've reached safety, you're supposed to shake off the excess chemicals because they're no longer needed. Wild animals do this naturally and efficiently. For example, if a rabbit outruns a coyote and reaches safety, it'll shake off the chemicals used to propel it away from the coyote. After this is complete, it'll resume its normal behavior without any signs of trauma. Humans have been conditioned to stop this process which is what causes the traumatic memory to loop within the system.

Most people aren't educated about how the system works, so they go home and think time will heal the situation. Some people will naturally process the situation and won't be traumatized. Others will not, and acute stress or post-acute stress will set in. This is where the system is constantly heightened, and the person struggles with regulating their thoughts, feelings, emotions, and behaviors. Trauma affects how you interpret yourself and the world around you. It defines your feelings, thoughts, and beliefs. Many people don't believe they have had any trauma. The problem with this is that when you begin to look at your reactions to your world, you'll most likely blame others or yourself. This tends to cause you to loop in blaming and shaming, which will keep you stuck in the belief pattern that's not serving you or your loved ones.

It can take years to accept that you've experienced trauma, especially due to the nature of how your mind and body operate. Most people come to see me when they've reached a bottom and they're unable to manage their lives and don't understand why things are happening to them. The guilt and shame become too great, and they can no longer repress their trauma. Even when this occurs, most people minimize their trauma due to the lower vibrating feelings surfacing when thinking about it or discussing it. There are also some who will overdramatize it in order to get the attention they felt deprived of as children. They tend to also seek sympathy and attempt to manipulate, which is another way to get what they think they need. Either solution is an attempt to solve a problem and meet their perceived needs.

Repressing trauma sets the stage for addiction, mental health challenges, and living in lack. I have never met anyone with trauma that hasn't struggled with some type of addiction or mental health challenge. This makes it difficult to respond to yourself and your environment in a healthy manner. Instead, it makes your system so sensitive that you're continually reacting to your environment instead of responding mindfully to it. It makes it impossible to experience the flow of life. Therefore, it's important to address past and current traumas. Otherwise, you'll not create the life you desire.

Stewart was struggling with relationships, addiction, and self-care when he started therapy. He was an army veteran of more than twenty years and deployed six times over the course of his service. He had also experienced childhood sexual trauma and neglect. He worked full-time for the government, was divorced, and had a young daughter under four years old when he started seeking help. He was highly intelligent and had read about specific modes of healing and had also gone to other counselors. Even though he'd sought help, he never engaged fully in therapy. He'd take the edge off and move on to battle things alone. He'd been in couples counseling with his wife for several years working through sexual issues, infidelity, and connection issues. He revealed he had an affair with a doctor who was supposed to be assisting him in attempting to connect more with his wife. At the time of this disclosure, he felt victimized by the doctor due to her position of power. The trauma Stewart had endured was intense and repressed to the point of causing major issues with his health, relationships, and mental and emotional stability. From his perspective, he was doing great, maintaining his job, and taking care of his responsibilities.

From the outside looking in, there were only a few visible things; his weight and skin condition. He continued to have sexual relations with several women—lying to them all—and struggled with sleep issues, overeating, and workaholism. He also indicated being sober and had attended brief treatment after being discharged from the military.

He repeatedly said, "I'm in no position to have a relationship. I have a lot of work to do. I don't have the bandwidth to handle things. I'm not taking care of myself."

Then he'd continue to engage in romantic relationships with women and deny they were relationships. He was also getting another master's degree during this time.

Every part of Stewart's life was filled with engagements, activities, and tasks. He seemed to be doing great things for himself, his family, and community, but when exploring things deeper, he was doing everything he could to stay afloat. His healthy behaviors were an attempt to repress his past and feel better about himself. Initially, his intentions were loving and kind. But they became a way for him to avoid his feelings of inadequacy. Every so often, he'd slow down and seem to engage deeper, then his trauma would surface, and he'd repeat the same obsessive behaviors. At the point of our last contact, he hadn't hit bottom. Hopefully, one day he will.

Going deep within yourself is important and something you won't regret. It's scary and difficult to face your deepest fears and release the pain from your past. It's also one of the most rewarding and satisfying things you can do for yourself. It takes consistency and diligence. We all have these skills within us. But not everyone will choose to use them and commit to having their best life. Some will decide to continue to battle like Stewart, and some will embrace all aspects of themselves and move through the pain. Either way, it's okay whatever you choose. It's your life, and you're the master of it.

Your body, mind and spirit are magnificent. We have just begun to understand how these systems operate and how to best support them. You're not your mind or your body. You're the observer of both. When you master this, your life will flow easily. That doesn't mean you won't have challenges. It means you'll be able to walk through them with grace and ease.

Chapter 6 Questions:

1. Before reading this chapter, how did you define trauma?

2. After reading this chapter and applying it to your life, did your definition of trauma change? If so, how?

3. Write about a traumatic experience you went through that's affected your life and how you connect with yourself, your loved ones, and peers.

4. Do you think it's possible to overcome trauma? Why or why not?

Chapter 7
Facing Fear

Fear is something we all experience on many different levels. It's a feeling, and just like all feelings, it provides information. It's neither right nor wrong, good nor bad. It tells you when to run, fight, fawn or freeze if you're in danger. It becomes an issue when you live your life from it: meaning your decisions are made from fear creating a fear-based life. When you do this, you become weighted down and literally create a self-imposed prison. This prison is based on protecting yourself, and when you're constantly worried about being harmed, you attract more harmful situations. It's easy to justify your stance when it's based on fear. Denial of the role you play in your life keeps you locked in and looping in a reality that's not supportive of growth and expansion.

Reaction Versus Response

Shakespeare said, "There is nothing more confining than the prison we don't know we are in."

The world is a mirror, and it reflects back to you what you're thinking and feeling. When you live to survive, you tend to be very reactive in nature which makes it difficult to respond and impossible to move into the natural rhythm of life. So it's imperative to learn to face it and move through it with as much grace and ease as possible. Many people struggle with admitting they're fearful. They declare they aren't scared even when it's obvious to everyone around them that they're very afraid. Some people experience shame when they admit they're afraid. Consequently, they move into anger or pride instead. These feelings are higher vibrating and tend to be easier to manage. Sometimes fear is covered by anger or pride because it feels better. When we're angry, we tend to feel powerful. When we are prideful, we believe we're better than others. That's why we reach for those feelings. There are many ways to repress fear as well as other lower-vibrating feelings. There are also those who vow never to feel angry and sit in pride or fear. But the common theme is to avoid fear and reach for anger.

Yet it all depends on your beliefs and how you perceive yourself and others. The key is to learn about yourself and your patterns and to identify what is underneath the surface driving your reactions. Learning to honor, embrace, and release the fear allows it to show you what needs your attention and gives you the space to respond and move into flow more frequently, which is the ultimate goal. ***Flow is bliss which supports peace within and around you.***

Fear becomes an issue when you live primarily from that space and make your choices based on it. This affects your entire life and greatly affects the happiness you experience. It's an interesting phenomenon because our society is fear-based and sells things based on fear, such as pharmaceuticals, age-rejuvenating products, food, and exercise programs to name a few. Fear-based marketing scares you in an attempt to get you to consume products. Granted, not all products are marketed this way, but a lot are because that type of marketing works. It lures people in to fix a perceived problem with an undertone of fear laced with a promised outcome of beauty. The more you're able to recognize your fear and let it go, the less susceptible you are to being manipulated into something that you really don't need or want to do.

Reaction Versus Response

This is also connected to your subconscious and unconscious belief patterns.

Years ago, when I was a counselor in training, I had an experience with an online coach that was a perfect example of this. I was struggling in all areas of my life, and I wanted my life to change. I had been in counseling and decided to try an online coach. I had read a book written by the founder of the program and was drawn to his methods and beliefs. Being an agency counselor was going to be tight financially, so I was looking for a solution. The coaching program I was attracted to was selling success and wealth, so it seemed perfect. I needed relief and that's exactly what was being offered.

When I called to inquire about the program, I was excited and scared. I'd been in school for more than six years and was recently married, and neither one of us was making a lucrative living. As the man started sharing the details with me, I felt anxious about the cost of the program. It was several thousand dollars, and I had limited income and was already in debt. After providing several appealing details, I signed up. During our conversation, I made the statement, "It comes out to having therapy once a week, so, it's definitely worth it." At that moment, I signed up. I was super excited about doing something new and felt confident that this would help me move through my struggles and create more abundance in my life. Then things took a turn for the worse.

I was on my first coaching call with my new coach, and at the end of the session, I discussed setting up future appointments. I wanted to get some on the calendar and possibly get a set day and time. During the conversation, she informed me I only had four total sessions, and the rest of the program was recorded interviews with the founder, worksheets, and other video tutorials.

I said, "What? The only reason I committed to this was because it was equal to having one session a week with a counselor."

She said, "That's not what's in your contract."

I was angry and scared. I felt taken advantage of and ashamed that I didn't realize what I was signing up for. I was devastated.

I gave up fighting the situation and made the best of it. I made the decision based on fear and lack. I was vulnerable at the time due to my situation and how I thought and believed. I didn't understand how my fear affected my decision. If I'd been confident and trusted that things would work out, I would've caught the pitch and been able to make a more mindful decision. This was a consequence of living life in fear and lack. For a while, it was easy to blame them, but then I had to take full responsibility for myself and my actions. I said "Yes" and signed the contract even though I felt fearful and uncomfortable during the situation. The fear was also telling me to stop and address it. I didn't. Attempting to overcome other fears, I ignored my current fear. Do you see the vicious cycle?

It was a great opportunity for me to learn. I couldn't say that then, but now I'm grateful it happened. That's why it's called growth.

It took me months to forgive them for not being clear and myself for acting out of fear. My journey acting from fear lasted much longer than a few months. It has been a gradual process learning to honor, embrace, and release my fear. I still experience fear just like everyone else, but it's much less intense, and I know I can move through it. I've learned to feel it and allow it to show me what I need to do, then release it. You can too. I can say with confidence that most of the people on the planet have lived life from fear at some point. If you're doing that now, that's okay. The key is to become aware of it so you can let it go and experience faith, peace, and joy too. ***Again, it's a process, and it's messy and imperfect.***

Fear controls us, and we use it to control others and our lives. Again, it's not a bad feeling, but it can be used to do bad things and to harm people. As discussed, you're more susceptible to being influenced if you're fearful, and you're more apt to attempt to influence someone else if you're in fear. That's why it's important to learn to manage your thoughts, feelings, and beliefs. As you become more aware of yourself, it becomes easier to contain your fear and allow it to guide you inward unless, of course, you're being chased by a tiger, then you either need to run, hide, or play dead.

As you continue to learn about yourself, your triggers, and what drives you, you'll be able to see your channels clearly: meaning, you'll be able to see what it was from your past being triggered in the present, making fear the common theme of your life. A life lived from fear is a life of survival. That isn't living. We all want to thrive, but most of us struggle with what that means and looks like. So I invite you to be patient with yourself, your loved ones, and your peers as you learn to walk this life in faith instead of fear. It may be hard at times, but it's all worth it in the end.

Chapter 7 Questions:

1. Have you ever been manipulated into doing something because of fear? If so, write about it.

2. Have you ever influenced a situation because you were fearful? If so, what was the outcome?

3. After reading this chapter, do you understand fear in a different way than before? Write about it.

4. Even though fear provides information, it can be harmful as well as helpful. How do you think fear is helpful? Write about specific experiences in your life.

5. How do you think it's harmful? Write about experiences in your life.

Chapter 8
Shame, Blame, and Guilt

Shame, blame, and guilt are normal feelings and are part of the healing process, just like all other feelings. Yet, they can be very destructive if not handled with care. The world today uses shame, blame, and guilt to influence you, just like it uses fear. Learning to honor, embrace, and release them is important for you to become a master at moving into the flow of life. These feelings, when not cared for properly, will keep you looping in the past and far from your highest potential. Shame is when you believe and feel something is wrong with you. Guilt is when you feel and believe you've done something wrong. Shame is much more intense for most people. When I've had shame attacks, I would get hot, start sweating, and want to hide. This used to happen to me all the time, but it rarely does now.

Reaction Versus Response

I've learned to embrace it and let it go. So when I experience it, it's less intense and less often. Once you learn to master your feelings, you'll still experience them, but you'll learn to allow them to flow through you instead of emoting them out at others and/or internally at yourself.

Most people know and understand that blaming is when you assign fault or wrong doing to someone, something, or a situation. During a shame attack, most people typically move into blaming to avoid feeling shame. This happens with guilt too. Have you ever called attention to someone's hurtful behavior, and they immediately said, "Well, you did it to me too!" They're flipping the situation onto you because they're unable to deal with their own feelings in the moment. That's why it's important to learn how to honor, embrace, and release your feelings. All of us, at some level, want love and acceptance from our loved ones and peers. So, learning to shift from continual reacting into responding and then eventually being in the flow of life supports you creating a life filled with connection and love.

There's no such thing as perfection in our world, even though many of us strive for it. It's exhausting to keep up with the Jones' and be something you're not. Agree? Again, feelings are messy. Thoughts and beliefs are confusing and conflicting at times for most of us. But they're also informative and important when it comes to moving into the flow of life. I've been blessed with an intense drive to learn new and helpful tools that make life more enjoyable. I've lived through a lot of difficult situations that have made me stronger. Yes, the saying is correct. What doesn't kill you makes you stronger *IF* you process your thoughts, feelings, and memories and change your belief patterns. If you don't process and let go of the pain from your past, you will become weak mentally, emotionally, physically, and spiritually. When you choose to stay the same and defend your position, you end up angry, resentful, sad, and depressed. This creates the breeding ground for intense continual reactions to life. That's not living; it's surviving. That's not what we're here for. We're here to live and thrive and help others do the same.

I was walking my dog one morning on a semi-closed trail near my house and encountered a man and his dog. Both our dogs were off their leashes, as many other pet owners do in this area. When we approached, my dog Ginger paused to make sure it was safe, and the man allowed his dog to approach

Reaction Versus Response

her. As soon as they met, they immediately connected and smelled each other as dogs do.

"Hello, I'm Susie.

"Hi, I'm Gary."

"How's your walk going?" I asked.

"Okay . . . part of it," he said.

Gary seemed shaken, so I asked, "Are you okay?"

"Yes, I'm okay," he said, then proceeded to share about how he and his dog Oley had run into a man with two dogs on leashes walking on the trail and how it turned into an altercation because his dog was off his leash.

"He was angry and wanted to fight. I'm seventy-two years old, and he was about thirty-five."

"I'm in no shape to fight, but I was afraid I was going to have to. He was angry and kept telling me I was a bad person and irresponsible. I got angry and said some mean things. It seemed over, but then he started following me."

He kept saying, 'We're going to work this out. We're going to shake on this no matter what.' I wasn't about to shake his hand."

I said, "It sounds like he had some other things going on, and he was taking it out on you. Especially since after he got angry, he was insisting on making things right even though it was in an aggressive manner."

Gary said, "Yeah, I guess I better forgive him and move on."

"That's probably a good idea," I said.

This was one of those moments I was blessed to experience because I was able to support this man as he recounted a difficult situation that elicited many different feelings and thoughts. He was shamed, guilted, and threatened for allowing his dog, who was old and walked very slowly, off leash. Gary was also angry and confused and wanted to maintain his stance for a bit because of the mere shock of the situation. He was non-threatening, and so was his dog. Yet the other man projected his fear, anger, shame, and guilt onto him. Basically, he was blaming him for other things that were buried within him that he was unwilling to work through. This is a major reason why it is important to learn and grow. Gary was able to let most of it go by the end of our chat. I'm unsure of the man he encountered, but hopefully, he concluded his behavior was incongruent for the situation and sought some forgiveness within himself.

Shame, guilt, and blame are feelings we all experience, and they're there to provide a pathway to what is hidden deep within the subconscious and unconscious mind. They're difficult to sit with yet rich with information that can lead you to a deep path of healing. Our society tells us to be afraid of these feelings and to shove them down. That is the absolute worst thing you can do to yourself. But that doesn't mean you should spill them out all over everyone, either. It means learning to contain yourself and give yourself the attention you need in order to have the life you desire.

Becoming adept at sitting with your feelings will help you move easily into the flow of life. Being in the flow is following the natural energy that is within and all around us. When you are continually reacting, fear will run your life. For most people, this leads to obsession, addiction, and mental and physical health issues. Flow is when you experience peace and satisfaction with yourself in the moment. You have a higher understanding that things are okay no matter what.

Colin Tipping wrote a wonderful book called *Radical Forgiveness*. This book goes into his process of forgiving others. One of the main parts of his process that I've noticed is vital to do and that many people skip, especially when they've had some recovery, is honoring your victim story. To let your victim story go, you have to honor it first: meaning you have to acknowledge it's there. That is what Gary was doing when he encountered me on the path. Initially, he seemed hesitant to share, but when he did, it flowed out of him. As he recounted it, he was able to let go of his feelings and move into forgiveness. It happened quickly and without prompting. I just said the truth of what I was observing, and he moved through it.

This is a beautiful example of honoring your victim story and moving into forgiveness which is freedom! If you hold onto your victim story and continue to loop in it, you will never heal or be free. What happens for a lot of people is they remain eternal victims and blame others for the state of their lives. You'll never get anywhere you want to go doing this. Yet you still need to feel the feelings and admit that you were victimized. After learning about recovery and taking responsibility for yourself on all levels, the challenge becomes honoring your victim story before you get to forgiveness. This one is sneaky and difficult for people who have already been down the healing path for a while because they've learned they have a part, and to let things go, they must forgive. The outcome is similar because the repressed feelings that were not released by honoring the victim story fully will surface in unwanted ways if not properly tended to.

As you can see, all feelings have a purpose and experiencing blame, guilt, and shame are helpful at times. They provide you with the road map to where you need to go within yourself to heal and release those things that hold you back. As you continue on your path, if you choose to expand and grow, you will become a master at sitting with your uncomfortable feelings as they surface. You may still stuff them at times—I still do—but you will move through them faster and be grateful for them. It can be difficult learning to navigate taking responsibility for thoughts, feelings, beliefs, and actions, but I promise you it's worth it. We're ALL capable of magical things no matter what we've done in our past. Yes, that means YOU.

Chapter 8 Questions:

1. Write about examples of feeling shame and how you dealt with it.

2. Explore the difference between shame and guilt. Write about examples of experiencing both.

3. Have you ever had a shame attack? If so, write about it.

4. Discuss a time when you held on to blaming someone for your situation. How did this affect you?

5. What are some ways you've avoided and/or repressed feelings of guilt or shame?

6. How to you forgive yourself and others? Write about your process.

Chapter 9
Emotional Intelligence: Wallowing versus Releasing

Are you emotionally intelligent? Do you know what that means? We live in a society that praises intellectual intelligence but doesn't promote emotional intelligence. We're taught to repress and suppress our feelings from an early age. Consequently, there are a lot of people on the planet with little to no emotional intelligence. You may have met someone who is brilliant intellectually, but when you engage with them further, they may be emotionally immature. Also, you may think you're emotionally intelligent and you're not. Emotional intelligence is being aware of your feelings and mindful of others' feelings, as well as being able to regulate, express, contain, and release them when necessary. Feelings are messy, magnificent, and connect us to our loved ones, to our experiences and to the past, present, and future. Feelings are necessary, but if they're not allowed to flow, they'll cause physical, emotional, spiritual, and mental distress.

When I became a counselor, we were taught to teach clients to identify their feelings using a feelings chart. We taught them to express them in a specific way. The main sentence was, "I feel this way (specific feeling) when you do this (behavior)." If you said "I think" and not "I feel," it was considered expressing a thought, not a feeling. That was the framework used to teach people to learn to identify and express their feelings. The issue was there wasn't a step about releasing them. I was teaching people to express and intellectualize their feelings which is exactly what I was doing in my personal life.

After years of therapy and healing work, I realized I wasn't moving through life as well as I knew I could. My intuition told me I was missing something. That's when I went to see a healer who introduced me to how to be with my feelings and allow them to flow through me.

As I started to practice this, I was able to move through life easier. So I started teaching this to my clients and noticed they changed quicker than before.

It's helpful to learn to identify what you're feeling. If you aren't good at this yet, then you can find feelings charts all over the internet that will help you practice identifying what you're feeling in any given moment. You can also use your body as a guide if you are connected to it. Some people are numb and struggle with this at first. If you're one of those people, start by identifying your feelings, then scan your body with your mind and see if you notice any sensations anywhere in your head or body. As you practice this technique, it'll help you become more connected to your body. Your body is your instrument to connect with your loved ones and your environment, so you can experience life to the fullest. That's why it's important to connect with what you're experiencing in your body. It's your guide and the link to your subconscious.

Learning to honor, embrace, and release your feelings is a huge step in moving into the flow of life. It's a process that takes time and practice. So be patient if you slip back into intellectualizing, repressing, or over-expressing. To honor your feelings means to notice they're there. Next, embrace them, which means be with them in the moment. Don't judge them or try to figure them out. Notice where they are in your body and breathe into them. Take as many focused breaths as needed to release them. Then, breathe in through your nose and out through your mouth. This can be difficult, especially with uncomfortable feelings that you want to run from, such as shame, guilt, fear, and anger, to name a few. Feelings have an electrical charge that cause reactions in your body. So releasing them with your breath before they have the chance to emote out into the world allows you to be more mindful and in the moment.

I consider intellectualizing, repressing, and over-expressing as wallowing: meaning you aren't dealing with your feelings. They're either being projected outward continuously, or they're being repressed in your mind and body.

Whichever way, you aren't honoring, embracing them, or releasing them. Wallowing causes looping conscious and unconscious thoughts. Thoughts create more feelings, and more feelings create more thoughts. Do you wallow in your feelings, or do you release them? I think most of us would say both. Feelings are beautiful and unpredictable. That's why viewing them as information instead of judging them as right or wrong is helpful.

Reaction Versus Response

This allows you to become more efficient at responding instead of reacting to yourself and others.

Paige, a previous client, started therapy to process her past trauma. She'd been sober from alcohol for more than seventeen years when she started sessions. She had also been in therapy years prior with several other therapists. When she began therapy with me, we started working on recognizing her feelings and how they connect to her reactions and inhibit her from being in the moment. Due to her severe childhood trauma, she was highly reactive and struggled. Quite often, she would dissociate into the past: meaning she would get triggered and react to her memories. Paige was emotionally immature even though she'd been sober for a long time and been in therapy. I've seen this occur a lot due to how most people are taught to deal with their feelings. As we gain understanding, it's easy to repress feelings instead of honoring, embracing, and releasing them. ***Emotional growth is stunted at the age abuse starts or at the age addiction begins.***

Paige was progressing in therapy when she decided to attempt to refinance her house. She didn't believe it was possible because she was retired and on a fixed budget. She'd been writing full-time for several years and was almost finished with her trilogy. She owned her home outright and was introduced to someone who could possibly help her get approved for a loan to get the equity out of her home. This would help support her financially as she finished her last book.

As Paige walked through this process, I walked alongside her and helped support her as she encountered many blocking beliefs and subconscious and unconscious fears.

In the beginning, she was ecstatic about the possibilities that were presented to her. After the process started, her fears kicked in, and she started obsessing.

At one session, she said, "I don't feel good enough. I don't make enough money."

At another session, she said, "I'm afraid if I do this, I'll lose my house. Then what will I do?"

As you can see, she was in a fear response based on past experiences that told her she wasn't worthy. The memories running in her subconscious mind were so strong that she believed what she was feeling and thinking. Consequently, her behavior became obsessive. As the situation progressed, she was able to let go of a lot of her past feelings and

Reaction Versus Response

shift her thought and belief patterns. This helped her walk through the situation with more grace and ease than she would have previously.

Paige stated, "This has been really hard, but I'm so grateful for the experience and what it's taught me."

Paige wallowed in her feelings, and she also released them. This is part of the process as you become more emotionally intelligent. You'll wallow at times and other times you'll release them. As you practice, you'll catch yourself quicker and move into releasing. Feelings are normal and connect us to ourselves, our loved ones, and all things. But they can also separate us from them when we wallow in negative feelings and thoughts. As you continue on your path, you'll continue to feel lower vibrating feelings. They don't go away, but they get easier to manage, and you'll eventually realize they're just information. The key is to allow them to flow through you as gracefully as possible and accept that some days will be easier than others. *You're human and designed to feel and think.* I invite you to commit to yourself that you're going to do your best to honor, embrace, and release those things that hold you back and forgive yourself and others to the best of your ability.

Chapter 9 Questions:

1. Write about a time you've wallowed in your feelings.

2. Write about an experience when you released your feelings. Did you use your breath or another method? Discuss it.

3. Was your emotional growth stunted? If so, when? Write about it.

4. Do you think you are emotionally intelligent? Write about how you are or are not.

Chapter 10
You Have to Feel It to Heal It

You have to feel it to heal it is a phrase I've heard many times in the recent past. I'm so grateful I did because I've learned how to feel my feelings and let them go before I fully emote them out into the world. Yet, at times, that still happens because I'm human and feelings are messy. Remember, as you continue to learn to regulate your feelings and emotions, be patient with yourself. We're all on our own path, and there's no time limit to get anywhere. If you put yourself on a schedule, you'll be continually disappointed because spiritual growth has its own *divine timing* for each of us. Do your best to allow things to flow. We're all human. Learning to forgive yourself any time you fall is imperative for growth and healthy connections with yourself, loved ones, and peers.

This isn't an easy task for most people, but it creates the space for more peace, love, and joy in your life.

During my first years of recovery, I was immature emotionally. I struggled to regulate my feelings and emotions. I would wallow in them all the time. As I continued to process my trauma, I realized I was crying old tears and releasing the pain from the past. Things started to clear, and I gained more power over myself. Yet, there was still a heaviness that I struggled with. It seemed that no matter what I did, it would never go away. I attempted to accept there would be continual suffering in my life no matter what I did. Not until I learned to honor, embrace, and release my feelings did things start to drastically change for the better. I thought I would always have a little bit of a dark cloud over me even though I was sober, in therapy, and doing healing work. I resigned to that belief but only for a short while.

I was eventually led to my current trusted mentor and healer, mentioned earlier Dr. Gary Cone. As I began the process with him, I noticed how calm and grounded he was. I sensed a peace within him that I hadn't experienced. As I continued working with him, I started to believe that I could experience the same thing. He helped me see there was a way to experience continual peace and love.

The interesting thing is I thought I had already found peace, but it was only bits of peace that I was experiencing. I thought I was just going to be emotional and misunderstood. There were a few other trusted mentors and healers who sat with me as I released old buried tears over the years. There were also many who shunned me for having them. When I started shifting my consciousness and living life instead of surviving, there wasn't anyone around who understood completely how to sit with and release feelings. It was about managing feelings and identifying them, as discussed in Chapter 9. It wasn't until years later that I learned I needed to feel my feelings to heal my wounds.

Learning to honor, embrace, and release your feelings can be a struggle because the mind wants to assign meaning to each feeling and then accompany it with other thoughts. That's when you start to wallow. Any time you sit with heavy feelings and breathe through them, they will clear. It's uncomfortable and may take several sessions with yourself to let things go. Don't give up. I still wallow in my feelings, but I catch myself much quicker than before, and I know I'm having feelings and that the thoughts are connected to them. Again, this is a skill. Learning to slow down, follow your breath, and meditate will help you implement this process.

Learning to meditate will help you become more adept at sitting with and releasing your feelings. Do you struggle with quietening your mind or sitting still? What do you do when this happens? We live in a world that tells us we must be constantly moving and producing to be successful members of society. This is a belief that breaks you down and severs connections you have with yourself and your loved ones. It's part of what creates negative belief patterns and low self-esteem in each of us. Learning to slow down and take your life back is imperative as you grow and learn to move into the flow of life. That's why learning to meditate is helpful because it teaches you to slow down, let go, and guide your thoughts. There has been a growing trend to meditate, and there are a lot of apps and guided meditations available for free and for purchase all over the internet. But you don't need anything except yourself and a place to sit or lie down and be still to begin experiencing meditation.

Implementing meditation into your daily routine is something that, over time, will change your life.

Reaction Versus Response

It helps you become the observer of your thoughts, feelings, and beliefs and assists you in becoming the best version of yourself. When practiced consistently, it can dramatically improve your life and your ability to change. It's learning to focus the mind and relax the body. Some people meditate on one thought, such as a positive affirmation or a spiritual passage, and ponder this concept as they follow their breath and sit quietly. Even though there are many ways to meditate, the main point is to focus and be in the moment. The world is full of distractions that keep you from focusing. If you don't learn to slow down and guide your mind and body, they will run off with you. That's when you feel you have no control over your life. When this happens, it's the perfect breeding ground for addiction and overindulgence in unhealthy things and behaviors.

Starting is usually the most difficult part when implementing a new behavior. We're so used to our routines that it can seem impossible to do something new. So, in the beginning, you may experience resistance to meditating. That's okay and very normal. But don't give up. I've seen so many people give up after only attempting to meditate once. When you learned to drive, did it take more than one try before you were good at it?

I can say with confidence that your answer is yes. So the same thing applies here. **Practice, practice, practice.** And do your best to make it an exploration instead of a job. Give yourself permission to be a beginner. It's okay if it's not comfortable or rewarding in the beginning. As you practice being still and calming your mind, it becomes a place you want to go. Granted, at times meditation is difficult even if you've been practicing for a long time. It's learning to allow the thoughts to float by your mind and get back to your breath. I would recommend using guided meditations in the beginning because you can focus on what you're being guided to do. If you start thinking about other things, that's okay, just move back to your breath as soon as you notice your focus has drifted. If you get frustrated, release those thoughts and feelings with your breath. Think of a toddler who has learned to crawl out of the crib. You must continually keep putting them back in until they realize they need to stay in there for a while. You may not have any resistance, and that's great. Either way, remember it's a skill. As you practice, it will become a part of you and your routine.

Every person I've counseled or mentored has struggled with feeling their feelings. It's a major issue that affects us in every area of our lives.

I've seen clients who would rather be deathly ill physically than feel the fear associated with a past trauma they're no longer experiencing. That's how powerful feelings can be if left unattended. The unprocessed feelings linked to the memories are stored in the body and mind. The emotional charge of these memories keeps them locked into the system. So, when you're triggered, you may loop in specific memories, thoughts, and/or feelings. That's why allowing the old feelings to be felt, released, and processed reduces the charge of the memory, helping the looping to stop.

A client I saw for many years did a wonderful job implementing these tools, and it changed his life. Howard started therapy for anger management and substance abuse. He had an altercation with one of his adult children that drove him to seek help. As he progressed in his process, he started practicing honoring, embracing, and releasing his feelings.

He said, "I keep forgetting to pause, feel it, and let it go."

After continually practicing in session, he started to remember to do it at home.

One session he stated, "It works! I sat with my feelings and they went away! It was much easier to talk to my wife afterward."

Before he started to implement his tools at home, he would wallow in his feelings and literally crash emotionally and would then act out with alcohol and anger. As he continued to practice his skills consistently, they became a habit. He shifted from his old way of coping to a new healthier way. His emotional dips were less intense, and he was able to move through intense conflicts without acting out. This dramatically improved the quality of his relationships.

As discussed in Howard's experience, it takes time to implement change. One of the biggest jobs I've had as a counselor is helping clients remember to implement their tools in their daily lives. This is because we're creatures of habit, and we struggle with change.

As mentioned in Chapter 4, patterns of behavior are programed in the subconscious mind, and one way to do this with a new behavior is repetition. That's why recovery groups tell you to attend meetings consistently and do the work outlined in each program, especially in the beginning. Also, when you hear something over and over again from the same person or different people in different ways, it programs the subconscious. You must release the charge of the memories tied to the beliefs in order to fully shift them. That's why it's important to practice, practice, practice honoring, embracing, and releasing your feelings.

What I've seen and experienced over the years is that some core beliefs change while others continue to float in the unconscious mind causing havoc on the system. Also, new limiting beliefs are programmed as you change. You're highly susceptible to information when you're in the change process because of the pain you experience from the behavior you no longer want to implement in your life. So be mindful of this as you move through your process.

Life is a journey and a process. It's okay if you choose harm-reduction methods over complete abstinence. **It's your life. It belongs to you**. Making choices about what's best for you is imperative. Changing for others never holds. You must change for YOU. As discussed all throughout this book, the tools shared are skills. You must practice them and make them your own in order to integrate them into your subconscious mind. Making them your own is beneficial when changing your patterns because you edit the tool or skill to fit you. You may not need to edit them, but you can if it flows better for you. Decide to make a skill or set of skills yours after practicing what works for you. Make them a part of you and release the ones that no longer serve you.

As you become a master at feeling your feelings, it'll be much easier to move into the flow of life. You'll learn to move with the natural energy that's within and all around you. When you're in fear and attempting to control your feelings and repress them, it becomes impossible to see clearly. All your senses become hijacked, and you're unable to see the beauty around you. It's impossible due to the skewed view you have of yourself and the world. So, if you want to enjoy life more and be more connected with yourself and your loved ones, practice feeling your feelings and letting them flow through you. It'll feel awkward and uncomfortable, just like any new behavior does. But don't give up. Make the tools yours. You have everything you need within you.

Chapter 10 Questions:

1. How were you taught to deal with your feelings? Journal about it.

2. Do you struggle with feeling your feelings? If so, what do you do to cope with them?

3. Practice noticing how you are feeling by scanning your body periodically throughout the day. Journal about it.

4. Do you believe everything you feel? Write about it.

5. Write about a time when you were out of control emotionally. How did you handle things after you calmed down?

6. Do you meditate? If so, great! If not, begin your journey.

Chapter 11
Relationships

Relationships are the cornerstone to growth and expansion. If you don't have others to play out your roles with, you can't expand. How you relate to others, animals, objects, and your environment is indicative of what you believe about yourself. We relate to everything in this universe in a specific way based on our thoughts, feelings, beliefs, and experiences. So that makes relationships extremely important to the human experience. That's why the stories shared about how others relate to their loved ones and peers help to show you how change takes place.

As discussed earlier, our core belief and behavior patterns are derived from our interactions with our parents, caregivers, and peers. They wouldn't exist if it weren't for these connections early on, as well as the ones made throughout life. The difference is that as adults, we have more freedom to choose who we connect with. The irony of this is that you'll gravitate toward those who are familiar, which will be healthy and unhealthy people depending on what's running in your unconscious and subconscious. Technically you think you have more freedom, but you're a slave to your own mind until you become aware of what's underneath the surface. That's why you react to your internal and external environments unconsciously. Therefore, it's important to learn about your early childhood relationships in order to become aware of the patterns that need to be changed and embrace the ones that don't.

Relationships are also about giving and receiving through the connections with people, animals, places, things, and/or experiences. Depending on how aware, unaware, open, or closed you are to connecting will dictate the depth of your relationships. Early in life, we're concrete and literal. That's why children struggle with understanding how adults speak to them. For example, when my son was four years old, while we were at the Science Museum he wanted a toy from the gift shop.

I said, "Okay, you can get something but not anything too expensive."

"So it has to be small?" he said.

"It depends on how much it costs. You have good taste, so you tend to pick things that cost more which is okay."

"And I smell good too."

I was tickled by his response as well as reminded of how little ones relate to the world. This is a perfect example of how children are more concrete and literal. My thinking immediately went to *he smells good* as if he were wearing cologne. And his mind was referring to how he takes in the smells of the world.

Another example of this is teenagers and how they're focused on material possessions they can acquire. They're still more in the physical and are concerned with status and connection through what they have, how they appear, and who they're associated with. This is very normal, and adults tend to get frustrated or judge children as they move through these stages because they've either forgotten they did the same thing or they have shame or guilt about how they behaved.

Reaction Versus Response

Understanding the developmental stages of childhood, adolescence, and adulthood helps you gauge where you are emotionally. If you have unprocessed childhood trauma, your emotional development was stunted at the age the abuse started. And if you started using a substance, or had a behavioral addiction start early on, this will also stunt your emotional growth. This leads to "little people grown tall," state of being, a phrase a mentor shared with me years ago. Basically, you're a grown adult with the emotional maturity of a child or teenager. Don't be alarmed by this statement. There are more people than you know who are emotionally immature. They may present as having it together, but most people struggle in this area because of the nature of our world.

As you continue to learn more about yourself and how your relationships reflect what's going on within you, they become more enriched and connected. A client named Adam, who came to therapy to address his addiction to alcohol and marijuana, transformed so deeply that all his primary relationships shifted completely. It was an amazing process. When he started therapy, he was angry and blamed his wife and children for his struggles, as well as his past experiences in law enforcement.

After continual processing, he was able to see how his loved ones were mirrors for his behavior as well as catalysts for his growth and expansion. He moved through his past trauma and shifted his belief system which enabled him to take responsibility for his thoughts, feelings, and beliefs. He learned to honor, embrace, and release his feelings which helped him become a better communicator. When he started therapy, he struggled with telling his loved ones what he needed. Instead of expressing himself, he would repress his thoughts and feelings and then explode during minor conflicts because of his stifled feelings. As he continued to practice his skills, he started to pause and respond. One day we were discussing communicating with his wife.

He was frustrated and said, "She doesn't listen to me. I get frustrated, and I shut down."

We explored how they related to one another.

He said, "She doesn't look at me. She's always on her phone."

So we discussed touching her shoulder to get her attention before he addressed her. He agreed to try this.

At his next session, he stated, "It worked! I've done it several times, and she heard me!"

After realizing that one of his core negative beliefs was "no one listens to me" and that he wasn't ensuring his wife was engaging, he was able to shift things within himself and take responsibility for his actions that feed an unsupportive belief pattern.

Prior to exploring his belief patterns and shifting them, he would wallow in self-pity and anger when he wasn't heard. As he realized he was the custodian of his own life and started taking responsibility for his actions and his reflections, his entire life changed. His wife started getting help, and his children followed.

It was one of the most magical experiences I've witnessed. I've been privileged to watch a lot of people change over the years but not many families take to the change as well as this one did. And it only took one family member taking responsibility for his life and doing the work for it to spread to the rest of the family. This also applies to everyone on the planet! When you do your work on yourself, shift your awareness, and be more in the flow of life, you will help shift others just by being alive. It takes work to have flowing relationships, and the work starts with you, just as it did with Adam.

He started the process, and then his family members followed. This isn't always the case, but it's possible for everyone.

Just as negativity can influence you, so can a positive outlook and a growth mindset. You are your most important project. Learning about yourself, letting go of the things that hold you back, and embracing the things that help you shine are part of the process. Relationships help you understand more about yourself and others. This elicits and supports change. As you continue on your path, triggers will diminish, lowering your tendency to react to your internal and external environment. You'll be able to pause and respond more frequently, even in heightened situations. Being in the flow of life will become an everyday occurrence. Remember to practice and be patient with yourself and others. We're all on this journey together—helping each other become the best we can be.

Chapter 11 Questions:

1. How do you relate to your family members? Are you connected or distant? Journal about how you relate to them.

2. Do you have a relationship that is distant that you would like to change? Write about your beliefs about the relationship. Is there a belief you would like to change that could possibly shift the connection in the relationship?

3. Write down and explore the beliefs of the relationships you believe are supportive and those you believe are not.

4. Assess how your relationships have helped you learn more about yourself, and what you want to change and what you want to maintain.

Chapter 12
Being in the Flow

Being in the flow is a deep state of surrender accompanied by trust in the divine essence within you. Do you believe you've experienced this? You have, even if you don't remember. When you were a child, you lived in this space until it was programmed out of you. Children live in the moment and are naturally attuned to their divinity. As we age, we forget who and what we are due to the conditioning we experience.

If you can take a moment now, imagine you're floating down a river without using an oar, and you're trusting the river will take you safely down the river. This is being in the flow. When you take the oar and start to steer and fight the current, you're attempting to control the outcome, and you're not in the flow of life. The key is to let go of any control you think you have and flow. It's a deep state of surrender where you know, feel, and trust that you're cared for and being guided through life. It is bliss.

Letting go of control is the hardest part for most of us. We're taught to control and to hold on in fear of what might happen. This also fuels being more reactive to yourself and your environment and doesn't provide the space to move into the flow of life. Since this is conditioned at a young age, reading this or even thinking of letting go may bring up feelings of fear for you. That's okay. It's not easy to surrender and allow yourself to flow with life.

If you have young children or grandchildren, watch them play. Notice how they're in the flow and using their imagination. They don't think consciously like adults do, and they go with what's in front of them. Being in the flow is natural to them. As we age, we're taught to schedule, control, and manage our lives so we can be successful members of society. As parents, we aid in this conditioning without knowing what we're doing. Before having children, some parents learn to let go and flow and allow their children more freedom. But overall, our world is set up to be controlled and to control.

So remember, letting go isn't easy. **You let go and flow, then you hang on and control.** It's part of the process.

We live in a consumer-based reality which tells us material possessions and products are what make us who we are. When we buy into this belief, we become slaves to the system and slaves to our thinking. We continue to seek things outside ourselves in order to feel whole and complete. This also includes spirituality and religion. When you're constantly seeking something, you'll never find it because it's within you. You have everything you need within you. But in the process of remembering this, you'll use your experiences with others and your experiences in the material world to step into your power. When something or someone becomes so important to you that you compromise your connections with yourself and your loved ones, you know you have misused your power and are being driven by the ego. You'll eventually fall or hit bottom, which is good because it leaves you the opportunity to expand, let go, and flow if you choose.

The belief that something outside you is going to complete you is a common belief that drives most people on the planet until they realize things can change. It's okay to have material wealth and an abundance of connections and experiences. It's your birthright to bring forth what you desire into this world. But when you become a slave to them and your self-worth is derived from what you possess or who you are with, you have abused your power and lost yourself.

If you believe something or someone will make you whole, you're living in lack within your mind. You'll seek outside yourself for what you believe you don't have, and you'll never truly find it. Satiating yourself this way will seem to be the solution, but after a period of time, this outward searching falters and you'll become restless and begin looking again for what you think you lack. This is the natural process for most of us humans. I've never met anyone who hasn't been through it or isn't going through it right now. It's a natural part of the life process. Some just choose to never fully move through it and others take the challenge and expand and grow.

The beautiful part is that once you've exhausted these avenues and hit bottom, you'll be ready to go within and remember the truth that you are whole and have all the things you need within you. That's what the questions, stories, and tools in this book are designed for; to help you remember your true nature and move into your birthright and live in the flow of life. Remember, it's not that life will be free of pain or reactions. You'll experience struggles continually. You'll never be completely free of your triggers. You're human; you have thoughts and feelings and beliefs, but you'll learn how to handle them in a different way that serves your higher purpose as well as the higher purpose of all things.

I had the privilege of walking the path with Cassie, a client I saw for many years. She learned to let go and live in the flow beautifully. She was consistent and diligent with her exploration and care for herself. Cassie started counseling to address her addiction to drugs and alcohol and continued therapy for many years after sobriety to improve her sense of self and shift her limiting beliefs. She worked through issues with family dynamics, past trauma, and codependency.

One of her main struggles was trusting herself and her own internal guidance system. She had always diverted her power to others especially to her mother and older brother. The interesting thing was they would always seek her advice. It was as if she was the family counselor. Yet for years she maintained a belief that they were more intelligent and aware than she was. As she started to become aware of this belief, she was able to improve her self-image and set appropriate boundaries. She started making her life her own.

As Cassie continued to release the pain from her past and shift her perceptions of herself, her life started to unfold in magical ways. Since she had been clearing her past for years, she was able to focus more of her energy on what she wanted out of life instead of processing her past. Releasing the energy from any reactions she had and moving into the flow of life were the focus of her sessions.

During one session, she said, "I have some interesting news. Sam got a job offer, and it's out of state in an area I'm interested in living."

As we discussed this further, she shared her goals and intentions that she had set several months earlier. She said, "I wrote down that I wanted to live by the mountains and live in a cottage-style home and quit my job by March. I can't believe it! Things are moving so fast! It's all happening at once! And it's exactly what I had intended. It's almost scary."

When she set her intentions, she was clear about what she wanted, and then she let go of how it would all unfold.

It was amazing walking through this adventure with her. Things continued to move quickly for Cassie she used her skills and embraced the fears that arose as the changes rapidly occurred in her life. She reacted many times throughout, but she was able to honor, embrace, and release her feelings and move back into the flow of life. She had become a master at responding to tough work and personal situations. This made it easier for her to let go, be in the flow, and allow the divine energy to bring forth what she desired.

Again, it was not without challenges, but she used the tools she'd acquired during her transformation process and embraced the struggles as they surfaced. Even though it was everything she wanted it brought forth discomfort because of old beliefs that she was able to shift during the process. This was a huge lesson in letting go, moving into flow, and following her heart.

Even after you master these skills, you will still react to things in your world. You're human, and humans have reactions. The goal is to react differently and become more aware of yourself in order to connect to the pure essence of who and what you are. As you continue releasing those things that hold you back, your relationship with yourself, your loved ones, and the world around you will become more enriched with connection and love. We're all here together to make each other better. Do your part and expand your consciousness and share your love with the world. ***YOU ARE MAGNIFICENT***.

Chapter 12 Questions:

1. How do you attempt to control things around you? Write about it.

2. Does it frighten you to let go and allow life to unfold? Or is it exciting or both?

3. Write about an experience where you let go completely and moved into the flow of life.

4. Observe children playing and notice how they're in the moment.

5. Practice on a daily basis taking a breath and noticing the sensations in your body. Then take another breath and observe the world around you for at least one minute. Allow your senses to take it all in.

www.ingramcontent.com/pod-product-compliance
Lightning Source LLC
Chambersburg PA
CBHW030305100526
44590CB00012B/523